MY FATHER'S
Wisdom
HIS DAUGHTER'S
Heart

MY FATHER'S

Wisdom

HIS DAUGHTER'S

Heart

A Collection of Recitations of
The Late George Carlton Hardy, Sr.
and
The Original Work of
His Daughter Kaye

Kaye Hardy Coates

Xulon Press

Xulon Press
2301 Lucien Way #415
Maitland, FL 32751
407.339.4217
www.xulonpress.com

Paperback ISBN-13: 978-1-6628-2805-8
Hard Cover ISBN-13: 978-1-6628-2806-5
Ebook ISBN-13: 978-1-6628-2807-2

A Collection of Recitations of
The Late George Carlton Hardy, Sr.
and
The Original Work of
His Daughter Kaye

TABLE OF CONTENTS

In Memory and Dedication

In Memory Of

My parents, Minnie Louise Spriggs and
George Carlton Hardy, Sr.
My sister, Patricia Bell Hardy Hannah
My brother, Ronald Lee Hardy
My niece, Pamela Ann Hannah Smith

This work is lovingly dedicated to my remaining siblings:

Joan Marie Morris
Doris Jean Savoy
George Carlton Hardy, Jr.
Sandra Elizabeth Hardy
Dolores Louise King

And Daughters:

Tamala Denise Sappington
Angela Marie Daly

For honoring the legacy of Mom and Dad and exemplifying the
true meaning of family.

FOREWORD

The original authors of these poems poured their own meaning into what they wrote so many years ago. Yet, Mr. Hardy brought his own uniqueness to these poems when he so eloquently quoted them, sharing with us his vast words of wisdom. The true value of sharing words of wisdom is that one would first apply them to oneself. The uniqueness of his quoting these poems is that they were the expressions of his life.

The author of this book now shares with you her heartfelt expressions and some original poetry in juxtaposition to the original works of art. It is my deepest desire that as you read this book, you will get a glimpse of the heart of the author and appreciate her unselfishness in sharing precious nuggets that personified the strength, wisdom, and essence of her father.

May this book be a source of comfort, peace, hope, and joy, and may you embrace these words of wisdom as a plumb line for your life.

"Words of wisdom are like petals thrown in a pond.
They continue to bring joy to the soul
long after the flower is gone."

Anne M. Whisonant, friend
Brunswick, Maryland

Acknowledgments

Recognition is given to the following (in alphabetical order):

Rev. Lueann Bethea
Rev. Dr. Michael A. Bethea
Rev. Dr. Pamela D. Blake
Evangelist Ida G. Brown
Deacon John Rodney Clark (deceased)
Mr. Earl C. Coates (husband)
Rev. Hedy L. Drummond
Rev. Richard T. Dyson (deceased)
Apostle Freddie Grant
Apostle Michael Grant (deceased)
Mrs. Eleanor "Lee" Hosby
Elder Vivian Jackson
Rev. Louis M. Kelly
Mrs. Sheila Kelly
Mrs. Diane Monroe King
Rev. Dr. George A. Manning
Dr. Virginia M. Manning
Rev. Donald L. Marbury
Mrs. Sheila Marbury
Rev. Clifton E. Sparrow
Mrs. Lyndra Sparrow
Mrs. Anne M. Whisonant

Each of you have greatly contributed to this work of love in your own individual way. A special "thank you" to Rev. Don Marbury, a fellow poet and author, for his guidance and critique. Collectively, your prayers, wisdom, advice, motivation, and friendship have been invaluable to me. Thank you, and God bless you.

From the Author

I was destined to compose this book. The inspiration came from my father, the late George Carlton Hardy, Sr. Therefore, it seems pertinent that I share with you a little about him. However, before we go forward, we must go back in time.

Many do not know this, but my great-grandfather, Dr. William Henry Bell, was born in Abyssinia, Africa. Grandfather Bell was enslaved and brought to America as a young man, along with his brother, to Jamestown, Virginia where they worked on a plantation.

Grandfather Bell and his brother were separated while working for a family of "Bells," from whom they took their name. His brother was sold on the "block" (an actual platform used by auctioneers to sell slaves), and Grandfather Bell never saw his brother again. Granddaddy Bell worked in the "big house" (meaning he did not work in the field, but served as a cook, a butler, or in some other domestic compacity inside the master's home), but he soon ran off to the North.

He joined the Union Army and fought in the Civil War for several years. After being discharged from the army, he went to school and became a teacher, moving back to Luray, Virginia, to teach. There he met Sara Elizabeth Strather, whom he married.

When Grandfather Bell heard about a job opening at Historical Storer College, he left Luray and went to Harpers Ferry, West Virginia, where he lived in the boys' dormitory (1882-1891).

Subsequently, he became a professor at Storer and was in charge of the boys. His daughter, Julia (my grandmother), and other siblings were born there. While at Harpers Ferry, his children were educated and graduated college. Afterward, he moved to Brunswick, Maryland, which was a booming railroad town, where his sons could get good jobs. After arriving in Brunswick, Grandfather Bell taught at Brookville School (nearby Brunswick). It was in Brunswick that Grandma Julia met and married George Albert Hardy. To this union, my father was born.

My father was born a proud Black American in the early 1900s—1912 to be exact. He came up in a time when family was valued, and godly values kept the family. He was married to Minnie Louise Spriggs, his devoted wife of fifty-eight years. Together they raised, trained, nurtured, and loved eight children.

Daddy was inducted into the armed services in January of 1944 and served in the US Army Air Corp during World War II as crew chief and aerial engineer. He was honorably discharged in December of 1945. As a civilian, my father worked for the B&O Railroad and retired in 1984 from the Chessie System after thirty-two years of service.

Pop-Pop, a name bestowed upon him by his first granddaughter, Pamela Hannah Smith (now deceased), was a gifted man, multi-talented. He played the violin, piano, organ, harmonica, guitar, and accordion (all self-taught) and, every now and then, you would hear him sing or whistle a melodious tune. Many in the Tri-State area (Maryland, Virginia, West Virginia) knew him as the "Mountain Lion," his CB handle.

Daddy was an intelligent man, educated and eloquent of speech. He was also a man of wisdom. I am not speaking of the knowledge he had, or of his intelligence, but of the gift he had for discerning and properly judging that which was right and true. He feared the Lord, which was the foundation of his wisdom.

In 1991, my father was honored at a special ceremony as one of Brunswick, Maryland's distinguished citizens. For this honor, he received certificates, awards, and letters of commendation from the American Red Cross, the Maryland State Police, Citizen's Watch, and Mr. Herbert R. O'Conner (who was once the governor of Maryland and a commanding general of World War II), all attesting to his years of dedicated service to the American people.

As a lifetime member of Ebenezer A.M.E. Church in Brunswick, Maryland, Dad, like Grandfather Bell, loved Ebenezer and believed in her mission to minister to the spiritual, physical, and emotional needs of all people by spreading the liberating gospel through word and deed. This characterized the hope my father had of a forthcoming Ebenezer. Although my father did not see the complete fruition of his dream, he and others laid a solid foundation upon which others could build to carry out the vision.

On Sunday, March 28, 1993, as the sun burned away the haze of the morning, my dad departed this life and gained his reward of eternal life. From Africa to America, from slavery to eternal freedom, the late George Carlton Hardy, Sr. (a child of God and an honorable Black American) left his mark on the hearts of many and a rich legacy to the world by the life he lived.

My father and the ancestors who preceded him were doers of the Word; rightly, I am destined to follow. Thus, this book was conceived from a seed planted by my father, but it has been born out of my love for the Lord and His people. In it, you will find a few of the many poems that Daddy would recite, some original poetry of my own, as well as the thoughts of my heart as given by the inspiration of the Holy Spirit.

Appropriately, contributions from the sale of this book will go to Ebenezer A.M.E. Church in Brunswick, Maryland, to aid in fulfilling its mission.

I pray that your spirit will be inspired, your soul stirred, and your heart warmed each time you visit the pages of this book.

Sincerely yours in Christ,
Kaye Hardy Coates
Servant of God

THE ESSENCE OF THIS BOOK

This book consists of fourteen soul-stirring poems. Subsequent to each poem, you will find the following four elements:

- From the Heart
- Food for the Soul
- Food for the Spirit
- Prayer

These brief, yet profound, elements were given by the inspiration of the Holy Spirit and provide words of wisdom for your contemplation.

- **"From the Heart"** shares the attitude of my heart as I reflected on each poem. I hope it will help you to open your heart to God.

- **"Food for the Soul"** is a summation of "From the Heart" and provides positive nourishment for your mind; it gives you something to think about. It is my hope that this section helps you to build strength of character.

- **"Food for the Spirit"** includes spiritual sustenance from the Word of God...precious provisions to feed and fortify your inner being. It gives credence to the "Food for the Soul" and anchors it in your heart.

- **"Prayer"** includes a succinct verse selected from the Book of Psalms. Although brief, the prayer offers a genuine way in which you can communicate with God.

It is my hope that each poem will speak to your mind, yet reach your heart. For that reason, I would suggest you begin with a prayerful request for revelation as you read each page. I fervently believe in Matthew 7:7 that says "Ask, and it shall be given you; seek, and ye shall find; knock, and it shall be opened unto you."

After you have digested the contents of this book, I pray that you will be satiated with godly wisdom and will know the breadth and depth of God's love.

...And He Said

THE TOUCH OF THE MASTER'S HAND

T'was battered and scarred and the auctioneer
Thought it scarcely worth his while
To waste much time on the old violin
But held it up with a smile.

"What am I bidden good folks" he cried,
"Who'll start the bidding for me"?
"A dollar, a dollar; and who'll make it two"?
"Two dollars, and who'll make it three"?

"Three dollars once, three dollars twice;
And going and—" But no,"
From the room far back, a gray-haired man
Came forward and picked up the bow.

Then wiping the dust from the old violin,
And tightening the loose strings,
He played a melody pure and sweet
As the caroling angels sing.

The music ceased, and the auctioneer,
With a voice that was quiet and low,
Said "What am I bid for the old violin"?
And he held it up with the bow.

"A thousand dollars, and who'll make it two?
"Two thousand dollars, and who'll make it three"?
"Three thousand once, three thousand twice,
And going, and gone," said he.

Then people cheered, but some of them cried,
"We do not quite understand,
What changed its worth," —Swift came the reply:
"The touch of the master's hand."

And many a man with life out of tune,
And battered and scarred with sin,
Is auctioned cheap to the thoughtless crowd,
Much like the old violin.

A mess of pottage, a glass of wine
A game—and he travels on.
He is "going once" and "going twice"
He's "going" and almost "gone."

But the master comes and the foolish crowd
Never can quite understand
The worth of a soul and the change that's wrought
By the "Touch of the Master's Hand." [1]

—*Myra Brooks Welch*
1878-1950

...And She Said

THE MASTER'S HAND

A brutal hand can leave a mark
That never fades away.
Scars that are deep, raised, and dark:
A reminder of harsher days.

Mental, emotional, physical marks
That humiliate, malign, and maim,
When unkind folk make hurtful remarks
With no regard for the one they defame.

Marks that leave one feeling shame
Bringing heartache, tears, and fear;
Inducing a sense of self-placed blame
Amidst hurtful stares and jeers.

But the gift of touch from the Master's hand,
To a life that is out of control,
Heals the wounds and loosens the bands
From a scarred and troubled soul.

For the Master looks through nail-scarred hands
Past the brokenness and debris
And gifts the touch that love demands,
Then sets the battered free.

—*Kaye Hardy Coates*

FROM THE HEART:

Often, we hastily evaluate people based on their appearances, or we pass judgment based on the trials we see them going through. In our haste, let us not misjudge one another and miss the intrinsic things that make us individually and wonderfully unique.

Human worth and significance are not determined by the external things we see. Our worth is determined by a loving savior who died on a cross to make something beautiful and worthwhile of our lives.

So, as we fix our eyes on the supposed imperfections of others, we must be careful not to let our eyes deceive us into underestimating their real value. For even the minutest thing has purpose and realizes its full potential when it is pliable in the hands of God.

FOOD FOR THE SOUL:

Events, circumstances, and situations have ways of touching our lives, revealing our inherent frailties. But it is the touch of God that perfectly reveals our inherent worth.

FOOD FOR THE SPIRIT:

"Therefore if anyone be in Christ, he is a new creature: old things are passed away; behold, all things are become new." 2 Corinthians 5:17

PRAYER:

Lord, "Keep me as the apple of the eye, hide me under the shadow of thy wings," (Ps. 17:8).

MY HEART SAYS

_____

_____

_____

_____

_____

_____

_____

_____

_____

_____

_____

_____

_____

_____

_____

_____

_____

...And He Said

A Psalm of Life

What the Heart of the Young Man Said to the Psalmist.

TELL me not, in mournful numbers,
Life is but an empty dream–
For the soul is dead that slumbers,
And things are not what they seem.

Life is real! Life is earnest!
And the grave is not its goal;
Dust thou art, to dust thou returnest,
Was not spoken of the soul.

Not enjoyment, and not sorrow,
Is our destined end or way;
But to act, that each to-morrow
Find us farther than to-day.

Art is long, and Time is fleeting,
And our hearts, though stout and brave,
Still, like muffled drums, are beating
Funeral marches to the grave.

In the world's broad field of battle,
In the bivouac of Life,
Be not like dumb, driven cattle!
Be a hero in the strife!

Trust no future, howe'er pleasant!
Let the dead Past bury its dead!
Act, –act in the living Present!
Heart within, and God o'erhead!

Lives of great men all remind us
We can make our lives sublime,
And departing, leave behind us
Footprints on the sands of time;

Footprints, that perhaps another,
Sailing o'er life's solemn main,
A forlorn and shipwrecked brother,
Seeing, shall take heart again.

Let us, then, be up and doing,
With a heart for any fate;
Still achieving, still pursuing,
Learn to labor and to wait. [2]

— *Henry Wadsworth Longfellow*
1807-1882

...And She Said

My Sacred Song

I pray my life sends forth a song,
Each note, each beat, each chord
Lift up a sound of sacredness
To God, my Savior and Lord.

I pray my life replicates a sound,
Vibrations traveling through the air,
Broadcasting a symphony of praise to God,
His greatness to declare.

I pray my life raises up an anthem,
A celebration of praise that freely flows,
Cascading down the "Rock of Ages"
God's power and glory to show.

I pray my life has a steady rhythm,
My heart beat like a drum,
A cadence of reverence unto my God
Until my life is done.

I pray my life, at its conclusion,
Be a spirited, musical tide.
The stanzas and all the crescendos
Be an operatic score for God.

This is my sacred song!

—*Kaye Hardy Coates*

From the Heart:

We are called to live a life of good works. Yet, no matter what good works we do or what great deeds we may accomplish, they are only imprints in the sand of time. How soon they are erased by the waters of life, unless they are committed to God. Ultimately, only what we do for Christ will last!

Food for the Soul:

Mankind seeks to pursue his ultimate dream, only to realize that he has lost sight of his true purpose and missed or forgotten his goal.

Food for the Spirit:

"Let us hear the conclusion of the whole matter: Fear the Lord and keep his commandments: for this is the whole duty of man." Ecclesiastes 12:13

Prayer:

Lord "...cause me to know the way wherein I should walk; for I lift up my soul unto thee," (Ps. 143:8b).

MY HEART SAYS

...And He Said

THE CLOCK OF LIFE

The clock of life is wound but once,
and no man has the power
to tell just where the hands will stop
at late or early hour.

To lose one's wealth is sad indeed,
to lose one's health is more;
to lose one's soul is such a loss
as no man can restore.

The present only is our own;
So live, love, toil with a will;
place no faith in tomorrow,
for the clock may then be still. [3]

—Author Unknown

...And She Said

TIME

To everything there is a season,
Distinctive periods of time
Pregnant with countless reasons
To fulfill a plan divine.

Crucial time for every purpose,
Vital time for every work,
A valuable gift given to us
By the creator of the universe.

Yet time can be a friend or foe,
Depending on how it is spent,
With power to produce joy or woe,
Determined by our intent.

Hopefully, we will carefully spend
The time we have been given,
For time on earth will have an end
And we'll reap of our decisions.

Our time will slip into remission
And life will end, no doubt.
What will be its fruition
When our time has all run out?

—*Kaye Hardy Coates*

From the Heart:

Life consists of moments of time. And, like sand in an hourglass, time has a way of quietly slipping through our hands. If we are not careful or attentive, today arrives and silently becomes yesterday.

According to Matthew 25:13, no man can pinpoint the time when the Lord will return. So, let us not put off until tomorrow our purpose for today.

Let us redeem the time by seizing the opportunities of the present to make amends for the missed opportunities of the past.

Food for the Soul:

Mankind considers time to be an inexhaustible resource...for God, it is. For man, the hourglass eventually runs out.

Food for the Spirit:

"To everything there is a season, a time to every purpose under the heaven." Ecclesiastes 3:1

Prayer:

"So teach us to number our days, that we may apply our hearts unto wisdom." Psalm 90:12

MY HEART SAYS

...And He Said

INVICTUS

OUT of the night that covers me,
Black as the Pit from pole to pole,
I thank whatever gods may be
For my unconquerable soul.

In the fell clutch of circumstance
I have not winced nor cried aloud.
Under the bludgeonings of chance
My head is bloody, but unbowed.

Beyond this place of wrath and tears
Looms but the Horror of the shade,
And yet the menace of the years
Finds, and shall find, me unafraid.

It matters not how strait the gate,
How charged with punishments the scroll,
I am the master of my fate:
I am the captain of my soul. [4]

—William Ernest Henley
1849-1903

...And She Said

UNCONQUERED

Out of the night, God has brought me;
From the prison of darkness, He set me free
To walk in His truthfulness and in His light,
With power, authority, and might.

I'm no longer indentured, though He masters me;
From bondage, He granted my liberty
To soar above the encumbering things
And the chaotic confusion that they bring.

I am unconquered! God set me free
From the shackles that came to restrain me.
And in my freedom, I've gained much more
Because the victor in me has been restored.

My life now affirms where He's brought me from.
By God's command, I have overcome.
Thus, in my living, I will make it known
It was by His power, and not my own.

I am unconquered!

—*Kaye Hardy Coates*

From the Heart:

The word "Invictus" is Latin for "unconquered," meaning to win by overcoming obstacles or opposition; to overcome by mental or moral power.[5] Invictus requires conviction and determination.

Determination is the act of definitely and firmly deciding a thing.[6] It proves to be a powerful motivator, especially when fueled with one's deepest convictions that come from the soul...that is, the mind, will, emotions, and attitudes of self.

Nevertheless, no matter how rigid the stance we take, when it comes to self, the victories are external and transient. True Invictus comes from God and brings victories that are internal, external, all-inclusive, and permanent.

Food for the Soul:

Determined self-reliance is not reliant at all! For that reason, let your motivation to triumph be dominated by righteous aspiration, not soul-ish stimulation.

Food for the Spirit:

"No, in all these things we are more than conquerors through Him who loved us." (Rom. 8:37) "...who gives us the victory through our Lord Jesus Christ." (I Cor. 15:57)

Prayer:

Lord, "I will never forget your precepts, for by them you have preserved my life" (Ps. 119:93).

MY HEART SAYS

...And He Said

CROSSING THE BAR

Sunset and evening star,
And one clear call for me!
And may there be no moaning of the bar,
When I put out to sea;

But such a tide as moving seems asleep,
Too full for sound and foam,
When that which drew form out the foundless deep
Turns again home.

Twilight and evening bell,
 and after that the dark!
And may there be no sadness of farewell,
When I embark;

For tho' from out our bourne of Time and Place
The flood may bear me far,
I hope to see my Pilot face to face,
When I have crossed the bar. [7]

—Alfred Lord Tennyson
1809-1892

...And She Said

CROSSING OVER

A time will come for crossing,
From earth and the things that vex,
A time for crossing over
From this life to the next.

A time for laying burdens down
And all we've suffered through,
A time for giving up the old
And taking on the new.

A time when hope is realized,
Our faith materialized,
A time of revelation,
As we bid this world good-bye.

So, before the time of crossing,
Put your hope in the cross
And choose this day whom you will serve
So your soul will not be lost.

For a time will come for crossing
From earth and the things that vex,
A time for crossing over
From this life to the next.

—Kaye Hardy Coates

From the Heart:

Life is a journey from birth to death. Much like ships on the sea, each journey has a final destination. Where we end is determined by the route that has been plotted, the preparations that have been made, and how we stayed the course. For the best passage and safest landing, we must choose Jesus as our captain and let the Holy Spirit pilot our lives.

Food for the Soul:

The journey of life clearly has a destination. Where are you headed? More importantly, where will you end?

Food for the Spirit:

"For I know the thoughts that I think toward you," saith the Lord, "thoughts of peace and not of evil, to give you an expected end." Jeremiah 29:11

Prayer:

"Lord, make me know my end, and the measure of my days..." Psalm 39:4

MY HEART SAYS

...And He Said

IF

If you can keep your head when all about you
Are losing theirs and blaming it on you;
If you can trust yourself when all men doubt you,
But make allowance for their doubting too;
If you can wait and not be tired by waiting,
Or, being lied about, don't deal in lies,
Or, being hated, don't give way to hating,
And yet don't look too good, nor talk too wise;

If you can dream--and not make dreams your master;
If you can think--and not make thoughts your aim;
If you can meet with triumph and disaster
And treat those two impostors just the same;
If you can bear to hear the truth you've spoken
Twisted by knaves to make a trip for fools,
Or watch the things you gave your life to broken,
And stoop and build 'em up with worn-out tools;

If you can make one heap of all your winnings
And risk it on turn of pitch-and-toss,
And lose, and start again at your beginnings
And never breathe a word about your loss;
If you can force your heart and nerve and sinew
To serve your turn long after they are gone,
And so hold on when there is nothing in you
Except the will which says to them: "Hold on";

If you can talk with crowds and keep your virtue,
Or walk with kings--nor lose the common touch;
If neither foes nor loving friends can hurt you;
If all men count with you, but none too much;
If you can fill the unforgiving minute
With sixty seconds' worth of distance run—
Yours is the Earth and everything that's in it,
And—which is more—you'll be a man, my son! [8]

—*Rudyard Kipling*
1865-1936

...And She Said

IF'S PROVISO

If sincerity is an authentic trait
that is housed within your soul,
Your life should be free of hypocrisy
Transparency should be your goal.

And if integrity serves as your moral guide,
And it governs your heart's desire,
Your life should be a model to others,
Truthfulness is therefore required.

And if modesty defines your daily walk,
And your speech shows great restraint,
Your life should display righteous virtues.
Moderation should have no complaint.

Then...

If you humble yourself before the Lord,
Walk upright in His Holy ways.
Well done will be your greatest reward,
An accolade from the "Ancient of Days."

—Kaye Hardy Coates

From the Heart:

"If" hints at uncertainty, yet it can bring about circumstances that afford us the opportunity to choose a specific course of action. The actions we take stem from inherent or learned traits that reveal our true character.

Character that is steeped in integrity, modesty, humility, and sincerity produces moral excellence that is not tainted by the "ifs" or uncertainties of life.

Food for the Soul:

It takes fortitude (firm courage) and humility to walk in integrity. How's your daily walk?

Food for the Spirit:

"I can do all things through Christ which strengthens me." Philippians 4:13

Prayer:

Lord, "Let integrity and uprightness preserve me..." (Ps. 25:21).

MY HEART SAYS

...And He Said

AN EVENING PRAYER

If I have wounded any soul today,
If I have caused one foot to go astray,
If I have walked in my own willful way,
Dear Lord, forgive!

If I have uttered idle words or vain,
If I have turned aside from want or pain,
Lest I myself shall suffer through the strain,
Dear Lord, forgive!

If I have been perverse or hard, or cold,
If I have longed for shelter in Thy fold,
When Thou hast given me some fort to hold,
Dear Lord, forgive!

Forgive the sins I have confessed to Thee;
Forgive the secret sins I do not see;
O guide me, love me and my keeper be,
Amen. [9]

> — C. M. Battersby (Lyrics & Music)
> Charles H. Gabriel (Arrangement)
> (1856-1932)

...And She Said

SUNSET ENTREATY

The day is done, the sun has set,
I'm headed to my place of retreat
Where the Lord and I have often met,
And I find His mercy seat.

A place where I beseech my Lord
To forgive me once again,
To bring me back on one accord
And forgive me of my sin.

And in His mercy, He hears my plea,
And gives ear to my solemn request
And I feel His love overshadow me,
As He bids my soul to rest.

It's in this place He shelters me,
In the covert of His wings,
And from the day's debris, He sets me free
And my soul is renewed again.

—*Kaye Hardy Coates*

From the Heart:

Each new day presents an opportunity to start afresh. Even so, as the day unfolds, we are also presented with temptations that could cause us to fall short of God's expectation of us.

As we ponder our motives and the attitudes of our hearts, we are required to empty ourselves of the debris of the day. Thus, our desire should be like that of David in Psalm 51:12 who said, "Create in me a clean heart, O God; and renew a right spirit within me." What a powerful way to end the day... with an examination of the heart.

Food for the Soul:

When we fall short, the Lord desires that we return to a "high place" in Him. Returning requires humility and repentance. Forgiveness is the benefit, which He freely gives.

Food for the Spirit:

"...If my people, which are called by my name, shall humble themselves, and pray, and seek my face, and turn from their wicked ways; then will I hear from heaven, and will forgive their sin, and will heal their land." 2 Chronicles 7:14

Prayer:

"Have mercy upon me, O God, according to thy lovingkindness: according unto the multitude of thy tender mercies blot out my transgressions. Wash me thoroughly from mine iniquity, and cleanse me from my sin." Psalm 51:1-2

MY HEART SAYS

_____

_____

_____

_____

_____

_____

_____

_____

_____

_____

_____

_____

_____

_____

_____

_____

_____

_____

_____

...Consider

Food for the Spirit...
Food for the Soul

Your relationship with God is a personal thing; so is becoming a Christian. It is about you and your faith in the work of Jesus Christ.

Romans 3:23 says, "All have sinned, and come short of the glory of God." The penalty for sin is death. Yet, John 3:16 tells us that "God so loved the world, that he gave his only begotten Son, that whosoever believeth in him should not perish, but have everlasting life." Therefore, no one needs to be condemned to death because "God demonstrated His love to us that while we were yet sinners, Christ died for us" (see Romans 5:8) "...the gift of God is eternal life through Jesus Christ our Lord" according to Romans 6:23.

As recorded in John 3:17, "God sent not his Son into the world to condemn the world; but that the world through him might be saved" so that "whosoever shall call upon the name of the Lord shall be saved" (see Romans 10:13). Therefore, according to Romans 10:9-10, "...if thou shalt confess with thy mouth the Lord Jesus, and shalt believe in thine heart that God hath raised him from the dead, thou shalt be saved. For with the heart man believeth unto righteousness; and with the mouth, confession is made unto salvation."

If you have opened your heart to receive the above truths, the following ABCs are for you.

    A cknowledge you are a sinner.
    B elieve that Jesus is the remedy for your sin.
    C onfess your sins to Jesus and receive forgiveness.
    D eclare Jesus as Lord and obey His commands.

PRAYER OF SALVATION

Dear God, I admit that I have sinned. I realize the penalty for my sin is spiritual death, which is eternal separation from Your loving presence. I acknowledge the only thing that can save me from this punishment is your grace. I believe and accept the work of Jesus Christ on the cross for my salvation. Therefore, I confess my sins to you. I am sorry, and I repent of my wrongdoings. Forgive me and receive me as your child. Amen!

Welcome to the family of God! This is what it means to be born again. John 1:23 says, "All who received him (Jesus), to those who believed in his name, He gave the right to become the children of God."

If you have prayed this prayer with sincerity, please consider the following four things:

1. Find a place of fellowship where you can be taught the Word of God.
2. Grow in the love, grace, and knowledge of our Lord, Jesus Christ.
3. Offer your substance and your talents for the work of the Lord.
4. Share your faith with others.

ABOUT THE AUTHOR

...God your love is immeasurable, your ways are deep, your love is unfathomable.

Reverend Kaye Hardy Coates: When you meet the author, it is obvious that the love of Christ emanates from her. Like her father, she is an articulate orator. She is gentle in character with a genuine love for people. As an encourager, she has the rare gift of putting people at ease, making them see the best in themselves, and inspiring them to greatness. Being in her presence gives one the sense of peace and well-being. As a result, everyone who meets her is immediately drawn to her.

Rev. Coates is the wife of Earl C. Coates, the mother of two daughters (Tamala and Angela), the grandmother of nine, and the great-grandmother of eight.

Born and raised in Knoxville, Maryland, she is one of eight children parented by the late George C. and Minnie L. Hardy. She attended Brunswick Elementary and High schools, graduating in 1969. Rev. Coates has attended Frederick Community College, Maple Springs Baptist Bible College and Seminary, and is a successful graduate of an intensive one-year federal management training program. A former employee of the US Department of Energy, she retired in January 2004 to pursue full-time ministry. During her long career at the Department of Energy, she received many awards for exceptional service, including the "Bronze Award," one of the highest departmental awards given for exceptional career service.

Rev. Coates is a long-time member of Ebenezer-Brunswick. She has a servant's heart and readily does the work of the Lord. This is evident by the many capacities in which she has served her church since her conversion in 1982. She was ordained in 1999 as a local deacon by Bishop Vinton R. Anderson (deceased) at the forty-ninth session of the Washington Annual Conference of the A.M.E. Church in Washington, D.C., and served as associate minister.

Since 2006, Rev. Coates serves as the associate pastor of Ebenezer. In conjunction with her customary duties, she is the author and coordinator of Ebenezer's Strategic Plan and the designer and publisher of the Church's website. Rev. Coates teaches Bible study and church school, serves as the quarterly conference secretary, and facilitates "The Gathering," a bi-weekly meeting of the Ebenezer sisterhood.

Rev. Coates is a multi-talented individual who unselfishly uses her gifts and talents to the benefit of others. The generous outpouring of herself and her resources is legendary. As a result, her compassionate and giving spirit has left its indelible mark on the lives of family, friends, and community. She is a visionary and an anointed preacher and teacher of the Word of God. She has been an invited preacher, motivational speaker, facilitator, and/or teacher at various church services, conferences, and retreats in Maryland, Virginia, West Virginia, Pennsylvania, Washington, D.C., New Jersey, and Florida.

Community-wise, she has served as a hospice volunteer and served on the board of directors for the Brunswick, Maryland Medical Center. She is also the founder and president of K.C. Ministries, Inc., a non-profit corporation organized to encourage and promote spiritual and personal growth and development, especially in women.

True to her calling, Rev. Coates is a faithful servant to her local church and community, but her overarching ministry is global by far.

ENDNOTES

1   Welch, Myra Brooks. "The Touch of the Master's Hand." *The Touch of the Master's Hand: With Ninety Other Poems,* Elgin, Illinois: Elgin Press, pages 15-16, 1941.

2   Longfellow, Henry Wadsworth. "A Psalm of Life." *The Knickerbocker/New-York Monthly Magazine*, Jan. page 189, 1838.

3   "The Clock of Life." Author unknown, n.d.

4   Henley, William Ernest. "Invictus." *A Book of Verses*, London: D. Nutt, pages 56–57, 1888.

5   Merriam-Webster online dictionary. https://www.merriam-webster.com

6   Merriam-Webster online dictionary. https://www.merriam-webster.com

7   Tennyson, Alfred Lord. "Crossing the Bar." *Demeter and Other Poems*, London, McMillian and Co., pages 174-175, 1889.

8   Kipling, Rudyard. "If." *Rewards and Fairies*, Garden City, New York: Doubleday, Page and Company, pages 181–182, 1910.

9   Battersby, C. M. "An Evening Prayer." *Awakening Songs for the Church, Sunday School and Evangelistic Services*, arrangement by Charles H. Gabriel, Chicago: The Rodeheaver Co., #107, 1918.

www.ingramcontent.com/pod-product-compliance
Lightning Source LLC
Chambersburg PA
CBHW072156060526
44654CB00046B/1320